Queen of Hearts
Hannah Hodgson

NEW**POETS**LIST

the poetry business

Published 2022 by
New Poets List
An imprint of The Poetry Business
Campo House,
54 Campo Lane,
Sheffield S1 2EG

ISBN 978-1-914914-22-5
eBook ISBN 978-1-914914-23-2
Typeset by The Poetry Business
Printed by Biddles, Sheffield

Smith|Doorstop Books are a member of Inpress:
www.inpressbooks.co.uk

Distributed by IPS UK, 1 Deltic Avenue,
Rooksley, Milton Keynes MK13 8LD

The Poetry Business gratefully acknowledges the support
of Arts Council England.

Supported using public funding by
**ARTS COUNCIL
ENGLAND**
LOTTERY FUNDED

Contents

For K,
Minute to Minute. We've got this.

Year 11

Secrets are like injuries from bullets. On entering the body
    there's a small entry point, on leaving
        there's a huge, open tunnel.

This is a tracing of deceit, as a lie grows bigger
    and bigger. He lied about having heart failure,
        told me this, fifteen minutes before

a chemistry exam. As I walk the winding path back
    to the start, the bullet's trace grows narrower
        and narrower, organs like obstructing hawthorn.

I re-examine the scene in which he told me,
    outside food tech, beside a bin. He produced
        a pill box and blood pressure cuff as proof.

How easily that bullet shredded me, his tongue
    an awful trigger. He left me bleeding
        for eight months. Eight months

of his pretending to be dying, whilst I actually was.
    I retained water, my skin tightening
        like a swimming costume drying

to salty crispness. He took that year from me.
    A year in which I should've been drinking
        blue wicked behind the cricket pavilion.

He forced hospitals inside of me before I needed
    a corridor linking my organs. Foreign objects
        are rejected by the body. Secrets, they always come out.

I Want to Tell Someone I Love Them

I was born in a bedroom drawer,
growing and growing until I moved
into the sink, the dresser,
the wicker basket by the fire.

Eventually I relocated to the fridge,
its plug ready for use
when doctors tell me
the terrible things they know.

I graduated from sixth form
into nothing, the space
where God was thinking
about creation, but hadn't

finalised his plans. I waited there
for someone to pluck me
like a fresh egg from the coop,
to crack my head and see

if I have a brain of double yolk.
I went through a phase
of sleeping on top of hedges.
My neighbours found me

on their hawthorn
and called my social worker.
I keep falling in love
with inanimate objects –

dearest, understand.
I wait inside wardrobes.
They're the closest replica
to the entrapment of a body.

Predators Beneath the Sand

Darkness has no bottom, as you get deeper
it crushes organs into dehydrated vegetables.

Bring me a submarine, dearest – place tanks of air
on my hips, tuck folded instructions into my bra.

Know that I'm in love, but that is not enough.
The sea creatures are eyeing me, my bowel an octopus

inside my abdomen, patiently
swimming in the dark.

The Paperback Version of this Body is Really Quite Flimsy

I use nail polish
        to stop my words
                laddering like tights
stitch my body into a washbag   so it can hold things
                cleaner than itself
I went to prison for cutting   my nails too short
despite the jury saying   bloody feet were punishment enough
        I put my camera in a holster
           and drew it like a gun
I licked stamps
             and stuck them
        onto the soles of my shoes
I placed a tracker   in my pen   and followed it to the dump
        I opened my window   and picked the moon
             like exotic fruit
        I filled a glass bottle with watches
and listen to their doom   impending

Beauty

Emptying a stoma bag is a transferrable skill –
an icing bag of shit piped down the toilet.

Summer is heavy in painful bones. Heat
and urgency, my body a car aflame

on a hard shoulder. When I get naked
for the first time with my girlfriend

she doesn't comment on my lingerie;
my body's lace of scar tissue too distracting.

When my life became a symptom
I became an informational campaign,

like those on the back of cigarettes.
My mother couldn't look at me without grimacing.

Tesco had given me priority delivery –
until I spent two weeks in hospital,

where I was briefly pronounced dead,
cancelling my slot automatically.

Exhibitionist

I peel my tights like a snake –
exoskeletons of mine gather
around the room, this museum
of self. Socks are mandatory
during sex due to the temperature
exhibits are kept at.

I've been diagnosed
with sixteen different stages
of deterioration. Each of these
ordered, like the process
of evolution, a poster
at the start of my exhibition.

I remove my syringe driver
from the display cabinet,
and connect it to a needle.
Somewhere, a doctor
is live streaming this
to his students.

Preparing a Body for Deep Sea Exploration

Sometimes, I only lose half of my consciousness.
The tide of pre-syncope swelling inside my mouth.

This is the purgatory of the body. A halfway border
towards consciousness. A mask knocked off,

a valve gone wrong. Only eighty seconds
before the body inhales water; mouth and nose

a convoluted party straw into the lungs.
An instructor told me to surface slowly

from unconsciousness. If you leave
too quickly, air expands inside the blood.

Sandbank gaps widen, capillary vessels pop,
The Bends happens. Always spend an hour surfacing,

to prevent weeks in a decompression chamber.
Snorkel in the shallows of your consciousness; enjoy the tourist trap

of this very specific darkness. Without hearing aids
you'll never hear the shark alarm.

Danger:

Records are written by strangers. Days are on repeat prescription.
Personhood is incinerated with laundry. Electric toothbrushes
have nowhere to charge. My body retreats and advances, tidal.
I do crafts with custard, cornflakes, and popcorn to show the doctors
I'm not food averse. Body lotion is confiscated, it contains alcohol.
Bleeps chirp in the nests of scrub pockets. Oxygen cylinders
drip like molten silver. PVC chairs, empty egg cups. A fruit stall
in the lobby. A 4% chance. Rows of patients side by side,
boxes of unlit matches. Fury gathering on lungs like pneumonia.
Doctors, wasps. Toddlers diagnosed with cancer. A Sellotape tin labelled
let's stick together. A hierarchy of pain. Pregnancy tests
before every X-ray. A single unpainted nail.

Fashion Always Comes Back Around

What my grandmother says about every 'new' outfit I wear

Inheritance is seeing a future you aren't guaranteed,
watching the antique market and hoping to become one.
The three of us are like fine bone china
manufactured at the same company, years apart.
We have an acceptance of the inevitable.
Yet still pretend heirloom cookbooks will fall to me one day –
that I will birth another beautifully pottered woman
who'll carry our faces in her backpack, and wear us interchangeably.

If This Were Read in Court it Would be Without Emotion

I found out I was dying and was pleased
to finally have an answer. My mother and father

didn't cry, but reportedly the clinic nurse cried
once she arrived home. My driving instructor

agreed I would never pass my test, just twelve hours
after I'd paid him for a further ten lessons.

My hair fell out, and I wasn't even sad
until I found a brand-new bottle of detangler.

My mother calls my disorder *minge*
because that's close to its actual name of MNGIE[1].

I've written a tiny book of funeral plans
but have no plans to show them to my mother.

We operate as a carriage clock, our minds
equal and opposite, unable to touch.

[1]pronounced m-nin-jay

Age Progression Software

There is a reason why I have never met someone
with smaller pinkie fingers than my own.

That my height doesn't follow graphs,
and my body is an anarchist. The same reason

why my mother loves plain Ritz crackers.
There is guilt attached to this knowing –

simple objects no longer have simple connotations.
My father ignores my body because he can't change it.

Instead, he's building a small flat
with electrical sockets in the ceiling.

My mother hangs her dressing gown
on the outside of the bathroom door.

If things are missing from her field of vision,
she forgets that they exist.

My brother is at university two hundred miles away,
and we're scared he's going to get someone pregnant

not because of the responsibilities or nappies,
but because it would have tiny pinkies also.

There is more to this than I can say here.
It's difficult to imagine my brother sleeping

with anyone. My mother is convinced
that he has barely given a girl a hug.

I allow her to operate in this untruth
because she uses it instead of sleeping tablets.

My father smokes instead of taking tablets.
When I'm with him he does so out of the side of his mouth.

I'm twenty-two and dying, but still my father
wants to protect my lungs.

Do you ever think about all of the photographs

A golden shovel

My body was like a motion activated light, every time I shat it took a
timer in my brain to switch off. Before surgery I was so full of gas that
was temporarily closed whilst I had my anus sewn shut. The
having sexual relations. I got my affairs in order, and by affairs, I mean
search for a girlfriend, suspending my Tinder account. After seventy-
stating *those who get on with it get better quicker.* They said I was
it prevents hernias. A nurse persuaded them to give me a single night-
I could sleep for four hours. The stoma bag itself was the metaphor.
with anything, people are determined for illness to be tragic. No one
my being more energy efficient, shitting silently whilst taking a Zoom
riff was given three scars like eyes with fused lids. A nurse moaned
and when I mentioned vibrators she laughed, cooing like a pigeon
and when I sobbed with homesickness/pain/tiredness she brought
two she said *fucking incredible.* I wanted to say all of the academic
percent of the world is born female, yet pain studies are conducted on
bodies are more likely to be prescribed sedatives for hysteria than
a physiotherapist's instructions, after two weeks I put on an underwired
on the nurses, as they taught me how to bathe my stitches at home.
the hospital. A healthcare assistant pushed my wheelchair to the
my mother was wearing gloves, a mask and a gown. In the car I
were read. Six weeks ahead of the surgeon's schedule I felt like the
bought an advent calendar of sex toys but opened all of them in
out of the house other than for surgery. I posted on social media
aren't a homogenous group, but wear a mask and save a life. The first reply

in which you're accidentally in the background?

while for **the**

the person in the next toilet cubicle would laugh. My **office**

surgeons suggested I leave sixteen weeks be**fore**

I stopped my **national**

four stitches, the pain team removed all opiates, citing biased **statistics**

entitled to three sets of spanx per annum on the NHS, as research **shows**

time dose so **that**

As

thinks **of**

call. My **mid-**

because her boyfriend was soon to partake in no nut **November,**

with the students. One student was nearly **twenty**

in nail varnish from home and painted my nails. *You're twenty*

things trauma had stripped from me, like **fifty**

males because the menstrual cycle alters results. Or femi**nine**

morphine for an open wound, but I was tired. As **per**

bra. The male doctor saw this as a huge step, and soon I was concen**trating**

Mum collected me at the entrance **of**

checkpoint, where because of **Covid**

switched over the radio channel when the day's **deaths**

owner, rather than the occupant, of my body again. I **had**

October. The year was closing, and I hadn't **been**

that *we the **disabled***

is *I'm going to find out where you live and invite infected **people.***

Convalescence in May

A translation & interpretation after Jules Laforgue

My body is an anchor on a seabed,
the blankets smell of industrial vinegar

and are damp with sweat. My ward mate
has a central line, a many tentacled device

in her carotid artery. We watch nurses attend
to us, so sick we're disembodied.

If this is death, I'll enter its darkness easily.
Here, regret scratches like hessian

and hell couldn't be this irritable.
I cannot let imagination extend beyond my destiny,

so these May evenings pass undisturbed;
my life unchanging, seasons my only movement.

The ward is full of little miseries, pretence
our friend – routine, the expected.

Is this the life my parents dreamed of?
They visit, smiling, pain unmedicated,

nor seen or heard. Their lives refashioned,
their souls canvases without painters.

On their way home, without sedative
hospital corridors they regain the unimportant –

the weekly shop, electricity bills, bin day. They phone
in the evenings, and I ache opiate-less.

It's a blameless ache, for if they didn't ring
I would hurt from lonesomeness.

My tongue is missing, waiting for me
to find and pin inside me like a medal. On this ward

my brain sits pickling in a jar,
self-pitying, trapped in the medical,

unable to extend to the metaphysical.
I lament the domestic, as the old lament youth.

Hospital its own country – how I wish
for doctors to grant me a visa home.

To be with my brother, counting the bricks of the church wall
instead of counting capsules. In my dreams I wander

along the coastlines of my imagination,
the sea lapping at my toes – how ready I am to go!

The caterers arrive and leave me nothing.
My roommate's boiled egg and camomile taunting –

she's dead on their arrival.

Colonel Mustard is Waiting in the Dining Room

If this ward were inside a country manor, it'd be hidden
behind a bookcase, switch activated, a BNF searched three times,
secret handshakes, drug protocols written on fancy menus.
Q Ten, Madame? Or Riboflavin for starters?

This ward is an inside joke. There are three seats
in the waiting room, and the table is immaculate.
That's how you know you're done for, see. When the staff
spend their own money on biscuits. Life here is Cluedo,

searching for weapons. *It's not the candlestick*, I say
it's never the candlestick here. There's no signage,
just two doors. One for bad news, the other for news so bad
there's a pale blue fabric sofa. We piss into prewarmed pots,

staff trying to pre-empt our every discomfort.
My grandfather broke his back catching an arsonist
who jumped. We specialise in living when we shouldn't.
Death between our teeth, a cold black flag.

The Mark Holland Trust

We wait to soften as vegetables must
in boiling water. The room so tiny

we jostle like circles of carrot, talking physio,
nutrition, drugs, pneumonia, the ring of white

soon to thicken on my brain scan.
We're told not to catastrophise

while we are boiled. Emotions seep out
like vitamins wastefully discarded

down the plughole. The room is steaming,
and soon we're dumped into the colander of home –

wet and fragile, separate entities
without the cohesive element of water.

Simply garnished, this body is ready for consumption.

Last Night, I Finally Remembered the Screaming

The waking, the pulling at sheets. Puddling into the mattress,
being absorbed by it. Naked. Gown too blood-heavy.

Blood in crevices. Anaesthetist administering ketamine,
wallpapering too quickly over my body's warning:

GET OUT in red pen over the plaster of my skin.
YOU ARE IN GRAVE DANGER. The glue is faulty,

it only held wallpaper for a few months. I pull
at peeled corners, run my finger through blood

still wet on the wall. The body remembers, offers clues
to the plastering underneath, I yank quickly, it isn't painless.

Breathing tube in throat, chest spluttering,
stitches buckling; falling fifty storeys,

expecting the floor in the next metre, the next metre,
the next metre, the n—. How sensible he was when saving me.

I have to. But don't worry, you won't remember this
and how I sank. How those drugs sank me.

I drowned and didn't resist. Three hours dissolving,
body sinking into the sheets like bread crust soaked

during washing up. The first thing I'm supposed to remember
is that I'm in High Dependency. The consultant

saying *things are as good as they could be.* Caution. Objectivity. Grit.
To slice and watch my unconscious, drip.

Not All Bombs Get Dramatic Conclusions

The foam cubes hiding wiring in the ceiling are liquid-stained,
and the ward sister stands on a stepladder every few weeks,
swapping them around so they match. The psychiatrists
point to the ceiling instead of inkblots. It's *blood* I say,
we're below a theatre. The drains backed up last night,
and we evacuated the ward. A kid shouted *By smelling shit
particles of shit are in your nose!* Until a nurse flushed
his nasal cavity with saline to shut him up.

The seated scales, the empty wheelchair, a confused man and his penis.

The codeine is fifteen minutes late, and a woman on dialysis
is screaming. *It shouldn't hurt* the nurse says, limping
on her stubbed toe. *I want all of this but beautiful* I say
to the matron, her uniform a bright, unread email icon.
The curtains are brown stained, saliva stained, conversation stained.
Hundreds of people have died on this mattress I say, and I am not one of them.
The man down the hall has an empty pipe in his mouth.
Dementia an orderly mouths, as if hiding this from a child.

Queen of Hearts

The bed wore me like a ballgown on a subway,
unignorable, melodramatic with its pleats of support;
the fancy clutch of a saline bag, the stiletto heel
of a drip stand. On this blank wall there's a signed picture
of Diana. They showcase her clothes in Buckingham Palace –
trapped ghosts of her hanging from clothes hooks.
Her terminal mistake was a man, while mine is contained
within this Hospice. I'm asked if I'd like to read her book.
The spine indicates nobody has read it through.
She'd approve of my need to get revenge on this body,
the ability to escape – health chasing me like a journalist.

Missing Posters

I was like a mother forgetting parenthood, leaving
her child on the bus. Did she go home with the strange man
who scowled and had a gold tooth? Or the pensioner who offered
to split lottery winnings with her, but never disclosed
who she was? *God, I thought she drowned* my mother said
fell through ice like a dog. The police never turned up,
but I keep her hairbrush in a Ziploc bag. Someday
they'll understand the seriousness. *I saw her hitching a lift*
my father said *I didn't stop because she looked feral, I didn't trust her.*
Her clothes are two sizes too small for me now. She is resting
in a shallow grave of fat. I search for her in the mirror.
I'm a blow-up version of myself; my valve belongs to someone else.

Clairvoyant for the Unconscious

When I faint, my mother talks through me
like a medium. *Hannah, if you can hear me,*
open your eyes. She calls in my dad or brother,
and instead of holding hands or chanting,
they carry me upstairs and place me in bed.
This is the space used to come back
from transparency, reclaiming autonomy
from the void. My blood gathers in puddles
around vital organs, oxygen trapped
in my compartments waiting for me
to wake, for the breeze of oxygen to leak
through the window seal of my brain
and rouse me like a cold drip.

Listen, I love you. Joy is coming.

Kim Addonizio

I envy the woman he carried out of fire;
because she's the single most valuable thing in her flat.

For nearly a year now I haven't been able to hug my father.
He navigates our home like a careful satellite –

when I enter the kitchen, he moves to the utility room,
when I'm in bed he hovers on the other side of a stud wall.

Pandemic firefighting has its challenges. Students hold up
their burnt pizzas from ten paces; there's a lack

of social distancing inside car wrecks. Once this is over
I'll surrender every candle he hates; embrace the familial equivalent

of a fireman's lift – saved from this awful void of space.

James Bond with a Stairlift

I encourage my mother to go walking.
To go and see her husband at the builder's yard.
To enjoy a scenic drive, or an impromptu visit to Aldi.
To phone her parents and get so emotionally involved

she couldn't possibly answer the door.
My mother is impossible to deceive – she can smell a plot
rising like cake batter in an oven.
She has read an article which says Covid can live

on a parcel for three days after being handled by the postman.
I see the red reflection in the window, and in desperation
I ring the landline with my mobile. I collect my box
while she scowls into the phone. I board my stairlift,

my getaway vehicle limited to one hundred metres per hour.
I alight, dragging my parcel and lock the bathroom door.
I fill the sink, add plain soap, and bathe my new dildo like a child,
holding her mechanical head above water.

A Family Christmas

After Caroline Bird

My stocking is filled with BBC Helplines that my mother has wrapped
in brown parcel paper. The Quality Street tin is disappointed at the
anti-climax of finally being opened. The radiator ejects snow and says
this is what everyone wishes for. The crackers contain prescriptions and
my brother is upset that he only got paracetamol. My great grandmother
comes down from the loft but instantly wants to go back up. My uncle
pours a kettle of boiling gravy over his head to hide his bald spot. The
tinsel is dripping because it's repurposed turkey foil. My advent calendar
has a tantrum because I'm no longer paying it attention. The tree has
become a toilet brush and is adamant that this is its dream occupation.
Santa has busted our faux chimney made of plasterboard. The candles are
melting themselves into revealing skirts. The television has gone home
to its family and left us. The scissors are self-harming, the living room is
filled with shards of metal. The hoover keeps farting and blaming my aunt.
The alcohol has removed itself from the room due to a conflict of interest.
My sister has announced she is a surrogate for a family of infertile mice.
My cousin has spent four hours screaming at the bathtub. The milkman
slipped on ice this morning and died – so today we have no orange juice.

Jesus Loved Men Too

I dated Christian boys so I didn't have to put up with them in bed.
Imagined women while kissing men inside the boiler room in the estuary.
I wrapped my sexuality in a wet wipe and tinfoil, like flowers
prepared the night before Mother's Day every year. And when I nearly kissed
my best friend I started humming to disguise my misstep.
I ignored myself to fit in with homemade biscuits after service;
to be the exact page number expected, to sing in a congregation
of repression. Our vicar left the Church of England upon legalisation
of gay marriage, and when I saw him in ASDA
he walked right through me, a miracle of mine, I guess.

What I Wish I Could Say in this Pandemic

I want to tell you I believe I'll survive this.
That I haven't been updating my will
or receiving texts from the government
as a 'high risk person'.

That dad isn't a firefighter. That six of his colleagues
haven't contracted the *C word* and are off work.
That he doesn't lie in bed pre-empting my death
and how it could be his fault.

I want to say people have been kind.
That we haven't had medical supplies
stolen by a delivery driver. Or that I haven't
been experimenting with vodka down my tube.

That I'm not existing in a vacuum of touch,
haven't tied my dressing gown tighter
to replace hugs. I wish I could say these things, but I can't.

Acknowledgements

Huge thanks to Suzannah Evans at The Poetry Business, for being a spot-on editor and lovely person. Thanks also to Katie McLean for the lovely typesetting and cover – it has always been a dream of mine to have a book which matches my lipstick!

My next set of thanks is double pronged. To Kim Moore, who was both a judge in this competition and a mentor of mine. Thank you for all you've done for poetry at large and your encouragement.

Thank you, reader. Your kind words and encouragement sustain me across platforms.

To my medical teams across the NHS. Thank you. Extra thanks goes to the Palliative Care and Hospice teams which oversee my care. Ironically, I've done a count and you guys have saved my life the most times out of any other specialism. Gold star! That's another misconception smashed as well.

To my family, thank you so much for your care and generosity. I hope this pamphlet (and my first full collection from Seren earlier this year, and my broken sleep pamphlet later this year) explains why my room is always messy…
(psst… reader… Do you think that'll get me off the hook? I doubt it somehow…)
I love and appreciate how much you've sacrificed for my safety throughout this pandemic. Thank you.

To my friends – I appreciate your kindness and understanding when it comes to both my creative and emotional ebbs and flows. I see you, and I thank you so much. Thanks also to Poety Group (not a typo), our space has allowed me to try out new things within my work and be kinder to myself.

The title poem, 'Queen of Hearts' was commissioned by The Dead Women Poets Society, as was 'Danger:'.

'Not All Bombs Get Dramatic Conclusions' won the Magdalena Young Poets Prize, judged by Fiona Benson, in 2021.

'The Mark Holland Trust' was first published in *Interpreters House*.

'What I Wish I Could Say in this Pandemic' was commended in the Young Poets Network x Bloodaxe competition; and is published on The Poetry Society website.

'Age Progression Software' was first published by *Butcher's Dog*.

'Convalescence in May' was commissioned by a project 'Reimagining Laforgue'.

'James Bond with a Stairlift' was published in *Brittle Star* magazine.

'Fashion Always Comes Back Around' was included in the Dove Cottage Young Poets pamphlet at Kendal Poetry Festival.

'Listen, I love you. Joy is coming' was commended in the Young Poets Network 'Love' competition and is available to read on the Poetry Society website.